Four Keys to Power

Fulfilling God's Vision and Plan for Your Life

by
Buddy Harrison

Harrison House
Tulsa, Oklahoma

Unless otherwise indicated, all Scripture quotations are taken from the *King James Version* of the Bible.

Four Keys to Power
Fulfilling God's Vision and Plan for Your Life
ISBN 0-89274-694-7
Copyright © 1994 by Buddy Harrison
P. O. Box 35443
Tulsa, Oklahoma 74153

Contents

Contents

Introduction

Unlock the Power

For years, there has been a misconception about power. People have thought, "It's evil to seek after power." Well, that can't be so, because Jesus says, "All power I give to you." (Luke 10:19.) And if He gave it to us then it must be good. What we must understand is that power is neither good nor evil until it is used. The way it is used may be good or evil, but power itself is neither good nor evil.

Take electricity for example. It can be used for good or for evil. It can bring you light, heating, air-conditioning and sound, but it can also give you the shock of your life and kill you. Does that make it evil? No, not in the least. There is nothing evil about electricity. Likewise there is nothing evil about power, but it can be used for good or for evil. It all depends on who is handling it and how they are using it. If power is in the hands of an evil man, then it will be used for evil, but power in the hands of a good man will be used for good.

So it is with the power that is in us as believers. We need power in our lives. We need power to be victorious in our marriage and with our children. If we pervert the power, then evil will come. But if we use it for good, then God will be glorified. Because you are a believer, you now have a dynamic power inside of you. Did you know that? God lives on the inside of you. He has invested in you. In other words, He has placed something good on the inside of you.

You may say, "But brother, there's evil out there." Yes, I know there is, but you can overcome it. You can overcome every situation, every circumstance, every trial and every test. How? With the good that is in you. You were made to be an overcomer. You have it in you. Don't let the devil tell you otherwise. Get a picture. Get an image. Get a vision of God living and working on the inside of you.

Some of you have had such a poor self-image for so long that you can't even see yourself being or becoming what God wants you to be. Eventually you must get to the place that you are absolutely persuaded that what He has promised you in His Word, He will perform. He wants you to have a powerful life. He wants you to have a powerful marriage. He wants you to have a powerful ministry. He wants you to have a powerful business. But you must do your part.

You must be determined and say, "I am going to be what God wants me to be. I am going to get in the Word and see how I fit into His plan and what His vision is for me and what steps I need to take in order to see it come to pass. This is a part of God's order for power in your life. If you don't follow His order, it won't work right. Because God is a God of law and order, He does everything decently and in order, and there is an order to receiving His power for your life.

When my two girls were small, Pat and I bought them some tricycles. Of course, they were the kind I had to put together. I had the instructions to go with them, but I didn't read them. I knew what a tricycle looked like. I had ridden one when I was a kid. So, I got out the pliers and screwdriver and started putting the pieces together. When I finished putting them together, I had three parts left over. It was then that a revelation began to come to me, "Something is wrong here." Isn't it amazing that we usually don't get a revelation until something goes wrong? Well, the revelation I got was simple but profound, "Go back and read the instructions!"

Some of you, like me, need to go back and read the instructions so you can put your life together following

God's order. Because He is a God of law and order, He works by *His* laws and *His* order. When you follow His laws and His order, then your life can be powerful. It can be effective.

When I get out of order with God, I can go back and tell you where His order broke down. At one point in my ministry, I went through five years of hell. I know it was hell because I could smell the smoke. I mean, it was chaos. I still preached the Word during that time, and people got saved, filled with the Holy Ghost and healed because God honored His Word, but I didn't experience the fullness of what God wanted. My life didn't carry the power that God wanted it to carry. Why? Because there is an order to things. When that order is violated, your marriage and your business won't be as powerful as they could be because they all operate based on a godly order.

So, if you want God's power to function in every area of your life, there are four fundamental keys you need to become familiar with. They are vision, communication, positioning and self-management. Once you understand these keys and begin to use them in your life and ministry, then you will unlock the power of God in your life and be able to fulfill all He has called you to do.

Key 1
See the Vision

Key 1
See the Vision

Where there is no vision, the people perish: but he that keepeth the law, happy is he.

Proverbs 29:18

In order to have a powerful life, you must have vision. If you can't see yourself living a powerful life, you will never have one. If you can't see yourself having a good marriage, you will never have one. If you can't see yourself being a success, you will never be one. To have anything in life — a loving mate, healthy family, prosperous business, successful ministry — you need vision. As Proverbs 29:18 says, **Where there is no vision, the people perish.**

What Is Vision?

Vision can have many meanings. In *Webster's, vision* means "something perceived in a dream, trance, . . . or supernaturally revealed." It also can refer to "a mental image," "mental acuteness or keen foresight," or a "force or power of imagination."[1]

According to W. E. Vine, there are three Greek words used in the Bible for the word *vision.* One word for *vision* means "that which is seen" and denotes a spectacle, sight or an appearance. Another word for *vision* refers to the "sense of sight" while a third word for *vision* is derived from a

---

[1]*Webster's New World Dictionary*, 3rd ed., s.v. "vision."

verb which means "to see, a coming into view."[2] So when you have a vision, there is something that is seen, whether it is a spectacle or an appearance, and something is coming into view.

So, when we speak of vision, it can carry a number of different meanings. My definition of *vision* is "insight into the plan, will and purpose of God for your life." God has a plan for all of us, and it is important to find out what that plan is, but we all need insight. We all need vision.

There is a parallel between natural vision and spiritual vision. Just like some people are nearsighted physically, there are nearsighted Christians. They only think of themselves. They don't care about anybody else. The people in other countries don't matter, and the people down the street don't matter. You can recognize them by their prayer life, which goes something like this: "Lord, bless me, my wife, my son John and his wife, us four and no more." When a whole congregation becomes nearsighted, the church becomes nothing more than a bless me club!

Some Christians, on the other hand, are farsighted. All they sing about is Heaven and their treasures over on the other side. They can't tell you what is happening here and now. They don't even know there is a revival going on and that the Spirit of God is moving right now. All they can say is, "Just wait until we go to glory. Over there we will not shed a tear." Thank God, I've got the beautiful hope of going to Heaven, but somewhere between over on the other side and what is right near me is a lost and dying world.

Instead of being nearsighted or farsighted, we need to have God's vision and find out what His plan, will and purpose is and pursue it.

---

[2] *An Expository Dictionary of New Testament Words* (Old Tappan: Fleming H. Revell, 1966), p. 190.

God's Vision Comes Through His Word

The Word of God is God's plan for you. It tells you His will. It is His last will and testament. Therefore, when you read the Bible you get insight into His plan, will and purpose.

To see in the natural, you turn on a light. It is dangerous to take action in the dark because you can get hurt. That is what the world does. They don't have a spiritual light shining, so they wander around in darkness and stumble getting hurt and killed.

The Bible says, **the entrance of thy words giveth light** (Ps. 119:130.) You are not going to see God's plan for you and God's best for you until you avail yourself to the Word of God. His Word brings light with it, and light is what causes you to see. Without light, there is no vision. You can be in a dark room and not see anything until there is some light. No matter how small the light, you will only see according to the light that you have.

So it is in walking with and working with God. You won't go any further or do any more than the light reveals. That is why we tell people that you have to get into the Word so that the Holy Spirit can come along and make it a reality to you. There is a difference between understanding something and it becoming real to you. When it becomes real to you, you will take hold of it and make it active in your life.

Many times we haven't understood that the Bible is the *logos*, the "sum of God's utterances."[3] His Words will bring light to you. Others can read it, and it is a dead letter. You can read it and not get anything out of it. But then, all of a sudden, you may be reading along, and a particular

---

[3]Vine, p. 229.

Scripture produces a hope, a confident or favorable expectation in you. The Spirit of God has shed a light on an individual Scripture which applies specifically to you. He has given you a specific word, a *rhema*.[4] A light begins to shine, and you begin to see.

Many times we haven't understood that the Bible is the *logos*, the Word that God has said. This Word will bring light to you. Others can read it, and it is a dead letter. You can read it and not get anything out of it. But then, all of a sudden, you may be reading along, and it produces a hope, a confident or favorable expectation in you. A light begins to shine, and you begin to see.

The kind of vision that I am talking about is a vision which is produced by God, that which the Spirit of God has spoken to your heart. Only when you get that light will you have sufficient faith to see the vision through. Without the light, it will just be a good idea that may never come to pass. When God speaks, the vision becomes a reality to you as an individual. It comes, not just as a hope or confident, favorable expectation, but as a reality in your spirit, in your inward man. You will begin to see what, when, where and how. You will have the directions you need to bring it to pass.

Get a Good Vision of God

But before anything, you need a good vision of God. Many don't have a good vision of God. For years so-called men of God have stood in the pulpit and told people that God kills babies and robs people of their businesses. As a result, people have a false picture of God. But when you read the Word of God, you get a different picture. The Bible says that Jesus **went about doing good, and healing all that were oppressed of the devil** (Acts 10:38). You get a whole different picture of God from His Word.

Rather than believing some men's testimony, I would rather take my vision from the book of light than from those

[4]Vine, p. 230.

who may be walking in darkness. I don't want to see God as they see Him. I want to see Him as He is.

Jesus was a living example of Who God is. Therefore, Jesus said, **he that hath seen me hath seen the Father** (John 14:9). Jesus was the Living Word. His life is unveiled and revealed in the written Word, the Bible. So when you read the Word, you can see His will for you. In 3 John 2 it says, **I wish above all things that thou mayest prosper and be in health even as thy soul prospereth.** In other words, it is His will for you to prosper and be in good health. To know what His will is, you have to get into the Word.

Some people think God is some kind of monster sitting up there on the throne waiting for them to make some kind of wrong move just so He can smash them. To them, He is like an old boy with a fly swatter just sitting and waiting for the flies to land. People like this have the wrong vision of God. They need to get into the Word so they can see Him as He is in His Word and begin to understand His character.

Get a Good Vision of Yourself

Along with a good vision of God, you need to get a good vision of yourself. Many people don't have a good vision of themselves. They see themselves as worms and say, "Poor old me." Some Christians don't ever get into the Word, so they don't know their value and have a poor opinion of themselves. In Romans 12:3, it says not to think of yourself more highly than you ought to think. But that tells you that you ought to think highly, not *more* highly. You have value!

When you hear the Word of God, you will begin to see who you really are and a right image of yourself will begin to form inside of you. The Word of God is like a mirror that reflects how God sees you, not how you see yourself. That is why you need to renew your mind with the Word of God.

When you do, you will be able to see yourself as God sees you.

According to Him, you are a brand new creation, a child of God. You are an heir of God, a joint heir with Jesus, a king, a priest, an overcomer, a victorious one. You are more than a conqueror and able to do all things through Christ. It is hard to keep feeling like a worm when you are hearing truths like that!

Then when you begin saying about yourself what the Word of God says, it begins to paint God's vision of you on the inside. But don't say it just once because faith comes by hearing, continual hearing. (Rom. 10:17.) If faith comes by hearing, then it only stands to reason that faith goes by not hearing. You say you don't see yourself the way God sees you? It is probably because you are not saying what God's Word says about you.

I don't know about you, but I get a whole different picture of myself when I look in the Word of God. I look better in Jesus than I do out of Him. Personally, I would rather see myself like He sees me than how my flesh wants to see me. My flesh wants to look at all my faults and shortcomings. It wants to keep me down. But because of the vision the Word of God has painted in my heart, my spirit man rises up, and I have a good vision of God and a good vision of myself.

Get a Vision of Your Future

Not only do you need to know who you are and Who God is, but you also need to know where you are going. Some people say, "Well, we're just going to go with God." Listen, God doesn't just operate on a hit and miss basis. He doesn't operate in a happenstance manner. As a matter of fact, He is the most organized individual you will ever meet in your life.

Have you ever read in the Word where it talks about your body as being marvelously and wondrously made? If you will just look closely, you will see that every detail has been tended to and that every part works together. In order for your life to move forward with purposeful direction, you must have a vision of your future and know where you are going. Some people are going in circles saying, "I just don't know where I'm at." Find out where you are and where you have been, and that will tell you where you are headed.

I am reminded of a story I heard about a scientific survey that was being done on processional caterpillars. According to this survey, you can line up these caterpillars, and they will just keep following the one in front of them. One scientist lined up some of these caterpillars on the edge of a pot and prodded them to get them going in a circle around the pot. In the middle of the pot, he put some pine needles. They went a whole day and night, a second day and night, a third day and night, a fourth day and night, a fifth day and night, a sixth day and night, a seventh day and night then fell dead out of exhaustion and hunger. The whole time they were within three inches of their food, the pine needles.

What was their problem? They confused activity with accomplishment. They aren't much different from many Christians I know who think that just because they are doing, they are accomplishing. In reality, all they are doing is running in circles. They are going around and around when what they need is within three inches of their nose.

Some of you are like those caterpillars. You are always busy, but you are not getting anywhere. What you need is a vision of your future. You don't need more to do. You need to have a vision of your future and make what you do count!

Determine Your Direction

Once you find out where you are and where you have been, you might find out that you need to change direction. How do you change direction? With your mouth. James 3:4 likens our mouths to the rudder of a ship. Even though the rudder is very small in comparison to the rest of the ship, it is the rudder that actually determines the direction that the ship will go. So it is with our mouth and the words that we speak. They ultimately determine the direction that our lives will take.

When I first started the church, every Sunday I would get up and tell everybody that we are a family church, a charismatic teaching center, and we are reaching the world. By doing this, I kept the vision in front of me and in front of the church. One time some visitors asked one of our people, "What does your church believe?" He responded by saying, "I don't really know what all the doctrines of the church are, but I do know that we are a family church, a charismatic teaching center, and we are reaching the world."

He may not have been able to talk about the doctrines of the church, but he did know what the vision of the church was. When the people in the church know the vision, then they can get in agreement with it and work towards bringing it to pass.

Consider What You Hear

What you hear will affect your vision. When I was in high school, I was on the football team. One time I was playing offensive guard against a team in Beaumont, Texas. I had to face this old boy who was 6 feet, 5 inches tall and weighed 265 pounds. Back in those days, I only weighed 154 pounds. I kept hearing that he was slow. My coach said that if I could get to him first that I would have the upper hand. All week long, my coach kept telling me that I could take him. When I watched films of him, I saw him as slow.

Finally the day arrived. When the other team lined up, I watched him on the practice field. When they called the signals, he was always about a half count behind the rest of the line because he was so big and clumsy. I had myself so programmed and ready on that first play that when I lined up across from him he looked just like a big tree that would fall over if I hit it hard enough. In my mind I said, "I'm going to hit him so hard, so fast that he won't know what has happened to him."

When they called the signals and the ball was hiked, I fired out towards him with every ounce of energy within me. He had just raised up from a set position when I hit him so hard that he turned a complete flip. That boy ran from me the rest of the night. Why? Because what I had heard had produced an image in me that caused me to go and do.

On another occasion, I played against an old boy from Baytown, Texas who went on to win a state championship. He was a line blocker who was only 6 feet 1 inch tall and 225 pounds, but he was quick and strong. Other guys on the team told me, "He's so good that if you don't watch out he'll eat your lunch." I heard what they said and saw it that way. When I came out on the field that night, he ate my lunch.

What you hear will cause you to see it a particular way. Ultimately it will be that way. When you hear the Word of God, it will produce an image on the inside of you. When you hear that God supplies your every need, you will see yourself out of poverty. When you hear that God is the Healer, you will see yourself healed. When you hear that He will never leave you nor forsake you, you will know that you are not alone.

When those words come to you and you hear them, they produce an image on the inside of you. Romans 10:17 says it this way, **Faith cometh by hearing, and hearing by the word of God.** It doesn't matter what circumstance you may have to face. You will react according to what you have heard.

If you have programmed yourself to be a failure, then you won't succeed. But God has no plan for failure. If He has no plan for failure, then we should have no plan for failure. There is no reason for us not to succeed. There is no reason for us not to win. What stops us? What we have heard.

Have a Big Vision

Once you do have a vision, let me encourage you to make it big. Why should it be big? If it isn't big, after a period of time you will lose interest in it. Do you know what happens to people when they don't have a big enough vision? They get whipped.

When I was in high school, I used to love getting ready to play against a real high-ranking team because as an underdog I could get all fired up. I could just see us whipping them. I could set a big vision. As an underdog, there was more intensity and more force involved when the other team was big.

Do you know why more big teams get knocked off by mediocre teams? Because they don't have a big enough vision. How many times have you seen some little old team that doesn't amount to much come along and knock off a big one, and the big one just struggled to be victorious? Why? Because they never set a big enough goal. What could they set that would be bigger than just beating a small team? Having an undefeated season.

That is what Christians do all the time. Because they don't have a big enough vision, they don't really have anything to shoot for. Somewhere along the way, if you have this small, little vision, you will be whipped because the devil has a vision of tearing you up.

Sometimes he will use people to get at you. They will tell you that you can't do this or that. They will tell you, "It can't be." People told me that I couldn't do half of the things I did. As a matter of fact, when I started to pastor all I ever heard was, "You've never pastored before. How will you do it?" Well, every pastor has to start somewhere, so in 1977 I came back to Tulsa and stepped out on the faith I had to start a family church, Faith Christian Fellowship.

I remember a discussion that came up one time with some businessmen. There was a big fund raising event. All of them were sitting around the table with me. Anyone of them could have given the money to get this particular organization out of the financial difficulty they were in, but they were discussing how they could raise the funds.

Finally one of the men, who was a millionaire, said, "Brother, how do you eat an elephant?" Some said, "Boil it and cook it down real good." Others said, "Fry it, and it will shrink." Everybody had a different idea on how to eat that elephant. When they all finished, he looked at them and said, "Fellows, you eat it one bite at a time."

Too many people look at something big and say it can't be done because it looks so big, yet they have never taken the first bite because it looked so big. Some people have come along and said that we can't build or that we can't do this or that.

When David went out to face Goliath, Saul told him, "You're nothing but a boy." Listen, David had been fighting for years. All the years of his youth, he had been a man of war. He had a vision. He had a vision of seeing that giant fall. He refused to be discouraged by what Saul said because he knew on the inside that the giant would fall, and he did.

Some of you have been faced with circumstances that look insurmountable, and people tell you that it can't be done. But if God has spoken it to your heart and you know that you know it will come to pass, then you can be sure that He will see you through regardless of what people may say or what the circumstances look like. God's Word says, **I can do all things through Christ which strengtheneth me** (Phil. 4:13) **and greater is he that is in** [me], **than he that is in the world** (1 John 4:4).

Be Realistic

There are, however, some visions, goals and dreams that are unrealistic, and they ultimately have a negative affect. I have kin folk my age that want to go out and play football with the younger crowd all the time. I can't really believe that I can go out and play football with those teenaged boys like I used to. I can stand out there and say, "I'm going to do it. I'm going to do it." I can be just as positive as I want to be about it, but if I don't really believe it in my heart, then it is a negative vision.

I am over forty years old and not interested in it. I'm tired and out of shape. I just don't have the faith that I could do it the way I used to anymore. If I tried, I would probably fall short. Why? Because I would have set an unrealistic goal for myself that I knew I could never reach.

Some people may say, "I'm going to believe God for ten million oil wells." That is big all right, but it also happens to be unrealistic. They have gone beyond what they can realistically believe God for.

When you build a building, don't you count the cost? Some people go into projects without sufficient faith to see them through. According to Hebrews 11:1, **faith is the substance of things hoped for, the evidence of things not seen.** So you had better find out if you have the substance to finish the job.

The Spirit said to me one day in tongues and interpretation through the Goodwins, pastor friends of ours,

"Do not enter into any venture until you have sufficient faith to see it through." Then he added a phrase to it that just got me, "Make yourself to see and to believe that it is My will."

Have you ever been where you couldn't see that it was His will?" You can't see because your vision is too limited. You don't have enough Word on what He has asked you to do. The entrance of His Word brings light. The entrance of His Word also brings faith because **faith cometh by hearing, and hearing by the word of God** (Rom. 10:17). You need the faith that comes from God's Word to see you through.

Get Into Agreement

When studying about vision, you also need to know about division. "Di" means two. Division is simply two visions. Let's look at division in the home. Division, or two visions, can easily come. When one of the children has done something wrong, the mother wants to correct one way and the father another way. They both have their own vision of how it should be done. As a result, confusion comes into the home. That is division.

That is also why a husband and wife should always consult with one another and take action together when it comes to handling the children. That keeps division from coming into the home.

How does division work in the church? God gives His vision to the pastor. If another in the church has another vision and keeps talking about it and proclaiming it, eventually it will cause division in the church. There can only be one vision in the church, and God will not leave His leadership out. He won't give the vision for the oversight of the church to someone else.

A church can't stay powerful when there is division. A home can't stay powerful when there is division, neither can a business. If you get two partners arguing about the business, one has one vision and the other has another vision, then you have division. It weakens the whole company, and it can't be what it ought to be. There can only be one vision in business, in the home and in the church. Why? Because we need the vision that God gave us so that we won't operate contrary to the laws of God.

When I first read Proverbs 29:18, the two parts of verse 18 seemed like separate statements to me, and I couldn't see how they went together. "But" is a conjunction so that means the two thoughts are tied together. But until I read the verse in a different translation, I didn't make the connection. The other translation reads like this: **Where there is no vision, the people run lawlessly; but he that keepeth the law, happy is he.** So it wasn't just a matter of perishing, but it was also a matter of operating outside of the laws of God.

The law of reciprocals says, "Where there is a vision, there is provision and the people do not perish." If there is no provision and if the people are perishing, there is no vision. Something is wrong. Insight into the plan and will of God is needed. Once that insight is received, agreement is needed. Vision is needed so that the people can operate within the laws of God and not perish.

Why Have a Vision?

Vision will help you look past your circumstances to the Word. Everybody faces circumstances. If you have a vision, it will help you to keep on going because you can keep looking to the vision. It will come to pass according to your faith, not your fate, not your fortune, not your feelings, friends or family but according to your faith.

I knew that our church was going to be big, but I also knew that there were going to be some obstacles to face along the way. It would be silly on my part to think that the devil is going to let me sail on by when his very nature is to steal, kill and destroy. To think that the devil is not going to bother me or try to rob my family or my church is presumption on my part. But if I know how to offset the devil and how to pray, then I can be victorious.

How can you offset the devil? With the tools and equipment God has given you — faith in the name of Jesus, the blood of the Lamb and the word of your testimony. By using the equipment God has given you, you can be an overcomer in the midst of every obstacle and every circumstance. But in order to be an overcomer, you must look to God when the hard times come. If you are struggling and having a hard time right now and you don't know which way to go, it is very possible that you are looking the wrong way.

I am reminded of a young sailor on board a sailing ship. On his first trip out to sea, he found himself in the middle of a squall. The waves were heaving high, and the boat was rocking and reeling. Then the captain sent him word to shimmy up the pole and set the sails.

As he was going up, he looked down and saw the waves rolling. He got nauseated and thought he was going to faint and lose his grip on the rope. About that time, an old sailor hollered up to him and said, "Look up, son. Look up." Instantly he obeyed that old sailor and looked up. His stomach settled, and he was able to complete the job. As long as he was looking in the wrong direction, he couldn't hang on.

Some of you can't hang on right now because you are looking in the wrong direction. You are in turmoil and don't know which way to go because you are not looking up. When you look at the circumstances around you, the wind and the waves, you take your eyes off of the One Who can keep you.

When Peter stepped out of the boat to walk on the water to Jesus, he took his eyes off of Jesus and began to look at the wind and the waves. What happened? He began to sink. He was unable to make it all the way. We aren't any different than Peter. When we take our eyes off of Jesus, we begin to sink and are unable to make it all the way. When we focus on Jesus and the vision He has given us, we will receive insight into the plan of God for our life and be able to look beyond our circumstances and move forward, to become mature, to be made real.

Key 2
Communicate Your Faith

Key 2
Communicate Your Faith

That the communication of thy faith may become
effectual by the acknowledging of every good thing
which is in you in Christ Jesus.

Philemon 6

The first key of the four keys to power is vision. It has to
start there because without a vision, you will perish. Don't
have a blackout. Keep the vision.

The second key to power is communication. To whom
do you communicate? First of all, you must have the right
communication with God. Some people only communicate
to God their gripes and bellyaches. If that is *all* you do, that
is wrong communication, and your vision will fall short.
Why? Because He doesn't entertain unbelief. **He that
cometh to God must believe that he is, and that he is a re-
warder of them that diligently seek him** (Heb. 11:6). He
wants to talk with you about His plan and purpose for your
life, but you must come to Him believing.

Secondly you must communicate with people. You
must speak the right words to people. In order to maintain
a good marriage, you have to speak the right words to your
mate. You can't say the good things just once. You need to
say them over and over. Even though my wife knows that I
love her because I told her I did when we got married, she
still wants to hear it everyday. She has a knowledge of it,
but if I don't keep saying it, she loses sight of it.

This is what happens in many marriages. They quit
speaking those words of tenderness, kindness and love.

They lose sight of their love for each other, and before you know it, they are pulling apart and can't even tell you why. What happened? They are no longer communicating and have no vision of the love and the bond that was there at one time. When they lose sight of it, the marriage loses its power to stay together and be effective.

Thirdly you should communicate to your circumstances. Why? Because when you communicate to your circumstances, it brings clarity. The more that you communicate, the more the light will shine and the more you will be able to see. If you continue to speak the Word of God and words in line with the Word of God, then you will receive clarity for your ministry, your marriage and your business.

Communication, More Than Words

Oftentimes when you think of the word, *communication,* you think of speaking. If I am going to communicate to you, then I am going to say something to you. But what you have to realize is that communication is more than just speaking or saying.

According to *Vine's,* the word for "communication" is the Greek word *koinonia* and literally means, in Hebrews 13:16, "be not forgetful of good deed and of fellowship."[1] It comes from the noun, *koinos,* which means "common"[2] and is akin to the verb, *koinoneo,* which is used in two senses — "to have a share in" or "to give a share to."[3]

Philemon 6 gives us some more insight into the kind of communication that we need to have in order to see our vision come to pass. It says, **That the *communication* of thy *faith* may become *effectual* by the *acknowledging* of every good thing which is in you in Christ Jesus.**

---

[1]Vine, p. 214.
[2]Vine, p. 90.
[3]Vine, p. 214.

Many times when you read a verse like this you have a tendency to just form a general picture of what he is trying to say then read on. But I began to do some studying on this particular verse and found that there is more here than meets the eye.

When you look at each word in the verse and the context the verse is in, you will get more of an understanding. In the context of verse 6, Paul is talking to Philemon, the slave owner, and is asking him "to give a share to" Onesimus since Onesimus was now a Christian. Now Onesimus, before he had run away, had stolen some money from Philemon, and Paul is asking Philemon to demonstrate his faith by forgiving him and receiving him back into the church in his home. Paul believes so much in seeing Onesimus restored that he even offers to repay Philemon the money that Onesimus had stolen.

So the word communication or *koinonia* means a little bit more here than speaking or saying words. It involves some action too. In other words, if he is a real Christian, he won't just give lip service to his Christianity, but He will *do* something about it.

This same word in other passages of Scripture relates to expressing our faith by ministering to the needy. (Rom. 15:26; 2 Cor. 8:4; 9:13; Heb. 13:16.)[4] There is no doubt that Onesimus would need some help from Philemon in some of the basic areas. He might need some food, some clothes or a place to stay for a while till he got his feet on the ground. Paul is encouraging Philemon to demonstrate his Christianity by sharing with Onesimus his resources.

Koinonia could also have been translated "communion." According to *Vine's* this translation in Philemon 6 means

---

[4]Vine, p. 215.

33

"fellowship manifested in acts, the practical effects of fellowship with God, wrought by the Holy Spirit in the lives of believers as the outcome of faith."[5]

When I pastored, there were a number of people who came to church that I called "Yeah, yeahers of the Word." They would say, "Yeah, yeah, I see what you are talking about. I see the vision. I am going to do that, yeah, yeah." But they never did it. They gave mental assent but were not committed. Jesus said, **Be ye doers of the word, and not hearers only** (James 1:22). You have to obey the Word and walk in it. Once you obey it, then the vision will expand.

Suppose, for example, that you get on an airplane leaving from Tulsa, Oklahoma. Once the airplane takes off, you can see further. When you begin to fly, you can even see beyond Tulsa. Why did your vision broaden? Because you began to act on it. You started operating in it.

The same thing happens in the spiritual realm. The vision won't expand until you begin to obey it, and the further you go in the vision the further you will be able to see. So when Paul is praying for them in this verse, he is praying that the communication — the sharing of their faith in actions as well as words — may become effectual.

Have Your Own Personal Faith

Notice that Paul is talking here about a personal faith, not another person's faith. There is a time and a place when you can operate on other people's faith, but there comes a time when you have to have your own personal faith.

My grandfather was an old Methodist minister that got filled with the Holy Spirit. He was a truly great man of God, and I really admired and loved him. As a boy I rode on his

---

[5]Vine, p. 215.

faith, and it carried me for a period of time. When I turned eleven years old, I was paralyzed with polio and was told I would never walk again, but he knew how to believe God. He knew how to pray the prayer of faith. When he prayed, he gave of the faith he had within him, and I was healed and walked out of that hospital a week later. As a boy I rode on his faith. I didn't exercise any of my own because I didn't know how.

Eventually though I came to a place in my life that I had to have my own personal faith. When it came time for me to accept Jesus as my Lord and Savior, I couldn't do it on granddaddy's faith. I had to have my own personal faith. According to Romans 10:17, **faith cometh by hearing, and hearing by the word of God.** When you get into the Greek and look at the word for *faith* that is used here, it carries the meaning that *faith* is "a conviction based upon hearing."[6] In other words what you have heard has produced a conviction in you, a faith in you.

I have a personal conviction that Jesus Christ Himself took my infirmities and bear my sicknesses and with His stripes I am healed. (Isa. 53:5.) That is a personal conviction of mine that I got from the Word of God.

Jesus had faith in the Father that He would raise Him up, would recognize His work and would bring us with Him as a result of it. I have faith in His faith. **I live by the faith of the Son of God, who loved me, and gave himself for me** (Gal. 2:20). He had faith because the Father told Him, "I'll raise you up." He had faith in what His Father said, and He was raised up. I have faith in His faith. I received my faith from the Word of God. I have faith that He raised Him up.

When the Lord spoke to me and called me to pastor, I didn't expect to be a pastor. I had no desire to be a pastor, yet the Lord called me and made it very clear. I knew what

---

[6]Vine, p. 71.

I had heard. At that moment the voice of God was real to me, and I came to a personal conviction in my own heart about what I had heard Him say to me. When He said, "You'll pastor supernaturally," His words became real to me.

I want you to know that I start services that way. I will declare it before the people. At the moment that I am communicating it, you become a fellowshipper in what He has said to my heart because I am communicating it to you.

When it comes to other people, you do the same thing. How many times have you heard Brother Kenneth E. Hagin get up and pray for the sick? Every time he will tell them that the Lord appeared to Him in 1950, that He placed His finger in the palm of His hand and that he has a healing anointing in his hand. Then he will lay his hands on them for healing. At that moment, Brother Hagin is communicating his faith. He is acting on what God said to him.

Because he has a personal conviction based on what he heard, he will speak it out and act on it. The more bold that he is the more that happens. The more bold I am to tell and to do what God spoke to my heart the more powerful it is. Whenever I do what God said, I am communicating my faith.

You are to communicate your own personal faith by sharing. You are to have a conviction based upon hearing from the Word of God or the Spirit of God that moves you to act on it. The Spirit and Word agree.

Put Your Faith to Work

Why should you communicate your faith? So **that thy faith may become effectual**. Notice the phrasing, **may become effectual**. When it says **may become effectual**, that means that sometimes it might not be effectual. Right?

The Greek word for *effectual* means "active, powerful in action." It comes from the same root as the word *work* which is translated *energy* in English. In Hebrews 4:12 this same word is used to describe the Word of God and implies that the Word of God is "full of power to achieve results."[7] Paul was wanting their faith to become effective.

How does it become effectual? By sharing it with others, not only in your words but also in your actions. When you don't do this, it is not effectual. It will not have the punch.

It is one thing to have a car, and it is another thing to have a car that works. People get all excited because God gave them an automobile. Well, glory! But does it run? That is how many people are. They have faith, but it isn't working.

Understand what I am saying here. You can have faith, but it has to work. It has to be active and powerful. Tell a teenager that you are going to get him a hot rod with a big 350 engine in it so he can just boogie on down the road. Watch his eyes light up. What is the point? It is very simple. It is one thing to have an old car, but it is quite another to have one that gets up and goes.

Unfortunately many people have faith like that. They have accepted the Lord Jesus Christ as the Savior of their lives and are even filled with the Holy Spirit, but their lives don't have any get up and go. They lack power. Their faith is not workable. It is not even active, and it surely isn't powerful.

Paul is praying that the communication of their faith may become workable, active and powerful. People want faith that gets up and goes. People want faith that works. Your experience with God may seem beautiful, but having

---

[7]Vine, p.19.

a beautiful experience isn't enough. You can play all the games you want, but when it comes time for the goods, people are looking for somebody who has a faith that is working, active and powerful. They don't want to play church. They don't want to play games.

Paul said, I don't come to you **with enticing words of man's wisdom, but in demonstration of the Spirit and of power** (1 Cor. 2:4). Paul knew who he was and what he had. He was even bold enough to say, **Be followers together of me** (Phil. 3:17). Some people say you shouldn't have people following you. Well, bless God, if they have sense enough to recognize you are following God, they will go with you.

I had sense enough to recognize that Brother Hagin was following God. Sure, I lost out on some things. My family turned their backs on me because I was following a man who called himself a prophet, but what they didn't understand was that he wasn't just talking a good talk. He wasn't just speaking and saying words. He was allowing people to share in what he had. When he laid hands on people, down they would go, legs would grow out and people would be healed. Now that got my attention. I could watch him and see that his faith was workable. It was tangible and real. It was active and powerful.

That is what Paul was wanting for them. He was wanting the communication of their faith, their personal faith, to be effective. Oh, you may look at great men of God and get excited. You may thank God for men like Kenneth Hagin or Oral Roberts. You may rejoice because of them. But, oh, how much better to thank God that *you* know the voice of God and that *you* are used of Him also.

Don't get your eyes on individuals. Begin, instead, to understand that *you* have a personal faith, a personal conviction based upon hearing. When you have heard it enough, the Word gets down inside of you. When you talk it enough, it is going to work for you. It is going to energize and empower you. It is going to charge your inner battery. And when your battery gets charged, you are going to charge somebody else's battery.

Acknowledge Every Good Thing

Notice the next part of the verse: **That the communication of thy** [own personal] **faith** [conviction based upon hearing] **may become effectual** [workable, active and powerful]. How? **By the acknowledging of every good thing which is in you in Christ Jesus.**

At Rhema Bible Training Center one day, the students were asking their teacher, Dr. Ken Stewart, some questions. One person asked him, "What does *acknowledging* mean?" Without thinking, he just popped up with the answer, "That's acting on the knowledge you already have." And that is a good definition. There are people who have knowledge, but they have never acted on it or done anything with it.

That word, *acknowledge,* is *epignosis* in the Greek. It refers to an "exact or full knowledge" which expresses "a greater participation by the knower in the object known."[8]

This same word is translated *knowledge* in Philippians 1:9 and Ephesians 1:17. In Philippians Paul is referring to a knowledge that displays itself in acts of love while in Ephesians he is talking about a knowledge that knows God in a deep and intimate way. The knowledge referred to in both of these verses is not the kind of knowledge that we can acquire through our five senses. Instead, it is an inner kind of knowledge we have about spiritual things. This spiritual knowledge is a fuller knowledge than the knowledge that is available to us through the five senses. It is this kind of knowledge that stirs up our faith so that it can be turned into action. The more we use it the fuller it will become.

---

[8]Vine, p. 301.

In the natural realm, my mother has developed her sense of smell. She has the best "sniffer" in town. She can smell smells that I never knew existed. There have been times when it has been very valuable to us. One time my mother smelled a gas leak in the house. Her sense of smell sent the rest of us sniffing through the house. The closer we got to it the more we could smell it. Finally we found it. Because she had cultivated her sense of smell, she brought us a blessing and may even have saved our lives.

So it is in the spiritual realm. When we put into use the knowledge we have of spiritual things, the fuller our knowledge will grow. Paul is referring to this same kind of knowledge in Philemon 6. It also comes from the Greek word *epignosis* and is translated *acknowledge* in the English. In this verse it is used in reference to "every good thing."

In other words you become effectual in the communication of your faith by having a fuller knowledge of and greater participation in every *good* thing which is in you in Christ Jesus. There are plenty of bad things going on, but if you keep acknowledging the negative, what are you doing? You are having a share in and giving a share of the bad things to others. He is not talking about the bad things here; he is talking about the good things which are in you. What good things? The good things that are in Christ Jesus.

Acknowledge His Presence in You

Are you in Christ Jesus? Then He is also in you. Colossians 2:9,10 declares that the fullness of the godhead dwells in you bodily. There is inside of you the Father, the Son and the Holy Spirit. If you have the full package, that is good. That is what you ought to be acknowledging, isn't it? That is what you ought to be recognizing. That is what you ought to be using. That is what you ought to be speaking and saying. That is what Paul was urging Philemon to acknowledge in himself — every good thing which is in him in Christ Jesus.

Acknowledge His Word in You

Have you ever had to go start one of those old Fords? You had to crank it in order to get it going. The more momentum you would have the more power you would get. Finally you would reach a certain point, and it would take off on you. That is what has happened to many Christians.

They hear the Word of God, and it becomes a personal conviction. They acknowledge it and recognize it. They begin fellowshipping in it. Soon they become a partaker of it, and it starts to generate down inside of them. Then finally they take off. They become active and powerful and begin to communicate their faith in actions as well as words.

That is how messages get inside of me. First I will get a thought. Somebody will be talking, preaching or teaching. Then all of a sudden, a word will jump up inside of me, and I will take off. I will start saying it to myself at the house. The more that I speak it, the more that I acknowledge it, the more that it will begin to work down inside of me. The more that I give place to it, the more it will churn and build and become powerful. It will enlighten me. When I say it and when I act on it, it will become clearer to me.

That is why I preach a message over and over again. It helps me. I begin to see it more clearly and understand it more. When I begin moving in that vein, revelation knowledge starts to flow out of it. If I didn't start preaching the knowledge I already had, the revelation knowledge would never come. Sometimes I will preach more revelation than I will pray out. While I am preaching, I will think, "I like that. That is good."

Acknowledge His Call in You

What do you have inside of you that can become active and powerful? Paul had a personal conviction. He had a personal conviction that he was to go to the Gentiles to minister unto them. Where did he get this personal conviction? When the Lord Jesus spoke to him while he was out there on the road to Damascus blinded by the light, he heard from Heaven. It produced a personal conviction inside of him that caused him to go out to every land. It caused him to activate and act upon the knowledge that he had inside him. It was the full and thorough knowledge that even the Gentiles could be saved. So he went and preached to them because he knew they didn't have to be held back. There weren't any limitations.

Acknowledge His Ability in You

Maybe it seems that you have had so many limitations in so many areas of your life. Where did they come from? From what you acknowledged and from the knowledge that you acted upon. You say you can't, and you can't. If you would say what the Word says, **I can do all things through Christ which strengtheneth me** (Phil. 4:13), then the power of God would be generated inside of you and would begin to go to work for you. It would become workable, active and powerful. You would begin to be affected by it and would say, **I can do all things through Christ which strengtheneth me.**

I used to walk into business deals feeling inferior because, at that time, I only had two years of college and hadn't graduated. When I was around people who were educated, my mind would start thinking the wrong way and would begin to say, "Boy, what are you doing here? You don't have the education or the training. Just who do you think you are?" I would have to go to work on my mind and start quoting 1 Corinthians 1:30, **But of him are ye in Christ Jesus, who of God is made unto us wisdom.** I would say, "I have the wisdom of God. I have the wisdom of God. Yes, I have it. I have it. What do I have? I have the wisdom of God."

All this time, I would be sitting across from the banker. He would be looking at me with a smug look on his face. My mind would be saying, "You don't have it." My heart would be saying, "You do have it." Under my breath, I would be saying, "I have the wisdom of God. I have the wisdom of God." I wouldn't feel like I had it, but by me acknowledging and acting on it, the power of God would begin to become effective inside of me.

I would make the statement, "I'll make the right decision at the right time. I'll do the right thing because God is in me." Then the banker would give his talk and advise me as to what he thought I should do. Then he would ask, "What do you want to do?" I would then tell him what I wanted to do. Afterwards he would say, "Well, yes, that's right. That will work." When I was leaving, I would hear them saying, "That boy is smart. He's a good businessman and sharp too."

If I had been going in the natural, I would have thought, "No way!" But when I turned the Word of God loose inside of me, the personal conviction that I had the wisdom of God inside of me became workable, active and operative in my life. I recognized that God was in me and that His Word would go and do what it said it would do. Therefore, there were no limitations.

As a matter of fact, the only limitations that I had were the ones that I acknowledged. The only limitations you have are the ones that you acknowledge. When you acknowledge them and say them, when you give place to them, then you are setting the limit. When you say you can't be healed, then you set the limit right there, and you won't go beyond that knowledge. Actually you can say anything you want to say and get yourself thoroughly convinced of it. You can school yourself into faith or out of faith by what you say. There is no question about that.

Acknowledge His Truth in You

But it takes more that just saying it to see it come to pass. I am not belittling confession. I am just trying to get you to see the other part of it. What you are confessing and having faith in must have truth in it. When you acknowledge every good thing that is in you in Christ Jesus, that is truth. He said, **I am the way, the truth, and the life** (John 14:6). He said, **. . . greater is he that is in you, than he that is in the world** (1 John 4:4). When you acknowledge truth, it becomes powerful inside of you. It becomes workable and active. It begins to work down inside of you and starts churning deep down within.

Act On What You Have Acknowledged

Then you are ready to go out. You are ready to say, "Bless, God, we're going to take this city. We're going to take this state, this nation, this world. There's going to be revival. I have a personal conviction that the people I lay my hands on are going to be healed. I am ready to acknowledge that *His Word is so* and that *God is the healer*. If you don't lay hands on them, if you aren't obedient to the Word of God, if you don't act on the faith inside of you, then you are held accountable. (Matt. 25:14-30.)

The only limitations that you have are the ones that you acknowledge. When you say you can't take the land, then you can't. When you say you can't go any further, then you can't. Where are your limitations? Where do you limit God? Maybe you believe that Jesus is your Savior, but you don't know if He is your Healer. Well, the Word says that Jesus Himself took your infirmities, bore your sicknesses and with His stripes you are healed. (Isa. 53:4,5.) Are you going to limit Him, or are you going to acknowledge Him?

Philemon 6 encourages us to acknowledge every good thing which is in us in Christ Jesus — His presence, His Word, His call, His ability and His Truth. When we acknowledge what He has placed within us, we will begin to do, to put into practice all that He has said, and His blessings won't be far from us.

Key 3
Get in Position To Receive

Key 3
Get In Position To Receive

And hath raised us up together, and made us sit together in heavenly places in Christ Jesus.
Ephesians 2:6

The third key to power is found in Ephesians 2:6 and has to do with positioning — being in the right place at the right time. You have to be in the right place at the right time for His blessings to come. And blessings only come when you are in a position to receive.

Have you ever decided to skip a church service and then had somebody come and tell you that you really missed out? They tell you about how the glory of God fell and about how they had a glory hallelujah time. What happened? You were in the wrong place, and the blessings didn't fall on you because you weren't in the right place for them to fall. Blessings are positional.

What happens when you are out of place? Trouble comes. Let me give you a quick illustration. Remember the account in 2 Samuel 11:1-17 when Israel was at war and David was so tired that he didn't want to go to battle, so he sent others out? While they were at war, he went on top of the roof, looked across and saw this good-looking woman bathing in the sun. To make a long story short, he lusted after her, had a relationship with her then sent her husband to the front lines of battle to be killed.

How did David get into that kind of trouble? He was out of place. He was in the wrong place. Where should he have been? With his troops. Why? Because he was a man of war. Instead, he was doing something he should not have been doing. He was in the wrong place.

What happens to people when they get in the wrong place? They get into trouble. Why does the devil want believers in the wrong place and out of position? So they can get into trouble. Why does he have that kind of attitude? Because he got kicked out of his place in heaven. He has been displaced, so he wants you to be displaced. Misery loves company. He is going through hell, and he wants you to go through hell too.

You need to get in your place. Whatever it is. You don't need to be out of place. If you try to become something you are not, the devil will tear you up. He will use it to start trouble. Some people say, "I don't want to do anything in the church." Others say, "I just want to be a doorman in the house of the Lord." Well, if that is where you belong then get there! That is where you need to be.

There is a church you should attend. Jesus is the Head of the church, and He will tell you where to go to church. You need to be where God wants you to be.

We think that we are free moral agents and that we can choose to go where we want to go. You just haven't prayed yet: Not my will but Thine be done. You haven't committed to God yet. You haven't said to God, "I'll go where You want me to go, be what You want me to be, do what You want me to do." You still have that stiff-necked spirit that says, "I'll do what I want to do." That is how you get in the wrong place and wind up in trouble.

You need to go to church where God says to go and work where God tells you to work, not where you want to. If you are supposed to be in the music program and you are sitting there like a stubborn mule, then trouble is going to come. Why? Because you are in the wrong place. On the other hand, there are some people who want to be in the music program, and they can't carry a melody. They don't need to be there. They are in the wrong place. If you want the blessings of God, you must be in the place that God wants you.

In Ephesians 2:6 we find that God has raised us up and made us to sit together with Christ in heavenly places. When we know our place, our position in Christ, then we will know who we are in Him and begin to act like it.

One day when I was watching the playoffs for the Super Bowl, I began to understand what it really meant to get into a position to receive. I remember watching the tight end on one of the teams go out for a pass. I saw him run a pattern and work real hard to get into position to catch the pass and make a touchdown.

I began to think about all the elements that went into catching that pass and wrote down seven things that, to me, seemed to be involved in making that play:

1) The guy had to get on the team,

2) develop the athletic skills and ability to be able to play the position of tight end,

3) get in position to receive that pass on that particular field in that particular game,

4) go far enough to win and be willing to pay the price,

5) shake everything else on the field off and get free to move,

6) look at the play coming at him face to face,

7) find the one special place for him to be.

Soon after I thought of an incident in the Bible that involved someone who used those seven points to get something from the Lord. An incident in the ministry of Jesus came to my mind. In the second chapter of Mark, we see a picture of an individual who has four friends who want the best for him, who want his life to be better and who will go to great lengths to accomplish that and see it come to pass.

And again he entered into Capernaum after some days; and it was noised that he was in the house.

And straightway many were gathered together, insomuch that there was no room to receive them, no, not so much as about the door: and he preached the word unto them.

And they come unto him, bringing one sick of the palsy, which was borne of four.

And when they could not come nigh unto him for the press, they uncovered the roof where he was: and when they had broken it up, they let down the bed wherein the sick of the palsy lay.

When Jesus saw their faith, he said unto the sick of the palsy, Son, thy sins be forgiven thee.

Mark 2:1-5

I think that so much of the time, as individuals, we have a tendency to not really go after the things we really need from God, much less the things we just desire. Most of us will not put forth the effort to get into a position where we can receive from God.

That man's friends had such a love for him and were willing to go as far as necessary to get him to the healing virtue of the Lord that they could not be stopped. They operated as a team, and they had to be mature and skilled because of what they did. They went into action. First they tried the door but could not get inside. They did not stop there as some people would have, but they were determined to go far enough to get the end result.

They were willing to pay the price of climbing on top of the roof, breaking up the roof — which probably was tile — and lifting their friend up in order to let him down to Jesus.

They could have gotten into trouble for breaking up the roof, and I am sure they probably had to go back up there and repair it. But at least they were willing to run the risk so their friend could have the blessing and the benefit of being healed.

We have a friend that sticketh closer than a brother also. (Prov. 18:24.) Jesus paid the price and was determined to make it all the way to gain back what Satan had stolen — the earth and its inhabitants. Jesus raised us up to sit in heavenly places, just as those men raised up their friend. Jesus gave us a new position — to rule and reign with Him. Their job was to get the man with the palsy into position to let him down through the roof. When they let him down, I believe he came face to face with Jesus and was in a position to receive healing. The goal of those men required great effort to achieve. It required diligence and determination.

If you want the blessings of God and all that He intends for you to have, you will need to exercise all of the elements those men did. You have to get on the team, mature and develop your skills, get in the action and go far enough to get in position. Then you have to get free of entanglements in order to win.

Get on the Team

The reason a lot of people have never received anything from God is that they have never really gotten on the team. When you come into the family of God and when you get to the place where Jesus is Lord of your life, there are certain rights and privileges that you will have simply by being "on the team," by being in the family of God. There always are certain rewards in life for just being a part of the family.

My children have certain rights and privileges simply by being born in my household. Although there will be other things that they will attain and gain for themselves in life, they have the right to receive food, to be protected, to be clothed and to receive the other benefits that come with being a part of a family. Then there are other things that they want which are extra, things they are going to have to do whatever it takes to obtain.

There are going to be certain blessings from the Father that you are not going to get unless you are in direct harmony and fellowship with Him. When my youngest daughter was preparing the final arrangements for her wedding, she and I went out shopping. We decided to stop and get some ice cream. We both had chocolate malts, and it was a delightful and refreshing time. My son was not with us, and we did not think to take any ice cream home. We finished our malts and did not want to leave trash in the car, so we entered the house with our empty cups and without any treat for him. My son had this strange look on his face. He seemed to be thinking, "I have rights. I am your child. Don't you love me too?"

This is the attitude of many believers when they see someone else receive blessings. They may think that God loves one person more than another. But this cannot be so because the Bible says God is not a respecter of persons. (Acts 10:34.) If I asked any parent which one of their children brings them the most joy, they would respond that it is the one who is obedient and who fellowships with them the most.

So I thought of how to reply to my son's look, and the only thing I could say was, "You were not with us when we bought the malts. It is not a matter of love; it is a matter of fellowship and of being there at the right time."

Until you are in a place of fellowship, until you are right there in His presence, you are not going to receive certain things from the Lord, even though you are His child. There are people who would love to see the supernatural power of God in manifestation, but they will not go to a place where it is in operation. They are children of God. They have rights and privileges, but they are not in a position to receive.

Remember the people at the Pool of Bethesda who waited for the angel to stir the water? Whoever was in position to get in the water first got healed. He was the one who got blessed. Time and again, we have wanted the better things of life. We have wanted God to work in our lives, but we have never put ourselves in position to receive from God.

Those guys who were playing in the Super Bowl got a certain amount of personal income simply because they were on the teams. Some of them, however, did not even play. Some of them never walked out there on the field, but the fact that they were on one of the teams entitled them to certain benefits. The team members who did not play on the field, however, did not get voted "player of the game," receive the praise for playing or have the personal satisfaction of accomplishment. There is a sense of accomplishment in knowing you have done your best and given your all. There is a joy in that.

Mature and Develop Skills

A lot of people want to have all of the benefits of those who go out to actually play, yet they have not taken the time to develop the necessary skills. In traveling around the country and talking to pastors, I see that attitude. Many of them want big churches and church growth. Some of them are willing to pay the price, and some of them are not.

Someone may see a pastor whose church is growing in what seems a phenomenal way and say, "I don't understand how he is doing that. You know, he has only been pastoring a year."

That pastor might answer, "Yes, but I was in the ministry fourteen years before that. I have learned some things about God and about church growth. I have sown some seed."

There may be others who do not want to study the Word or invest time working in an already established ministry while waiting for God to move them into place as He sees their skills develop. Then they wonder why their churches do not prosper.

There is a time element involved in maturing and in developing skills, just as sharpening a knife or an axe to a fine edge so that it works better than ordinary axes. Even in rookie athletes, you can see this principle. It takes them a period of time to develop, to cultivate skills, to play in different positions until the time comes when they have matured and developed and are ready for the front running positions.

A lot of people do not want to take that time to mature, to be considered of good enough quality to replace the quality players ahead of them. A lot of people would like to be another Kenneth Hagin, but they are not willing to pay the price he paid.

You may say, "Well, it is not required of me to pay the same price." But it is required of you to have the same knowledge and spiritual development to get to the same place. Maybe you can do it faster than he did because of all his knowledge you now have to build on that he did not have in the beginning. Just as with athletes today, there are weight-lifting programs that build muscles faster and quicker now than was possible twenty years ago, but you still have to build muscles. You can't skip any of the steps to getting in the right condition even though some may be able to go through those steps faster than others.

Get in the Action

A lot of people never bother to get in the action. The quarterback can call the signals, and you can stand there at the line and never move. As a Christian, you can do the same thing and never be in a position to receive certain rewards because you don't go. A lot of people are still at the starting line. They have never moved out, never moved one peg, never made any effort whatsoever. They have developed the maturity and the skills, but they are still sitting there. That inactivity will stop them from getting in position. It is vital to have action, to be moving.

A lot of people get in the action, but when the going gets a little rough, they back up or quit. Anything you take on that is sizable will bring somebody to take pot shots at you. Many times it will be Christians who do not have sense enough to know they are being used of the devil. They may be coming at you from every direction. But it will not stop you or alter your direction if you have determined to accomplish the goal God has set before you.

Go All the Way

Now if a tight end is going to get a first down or a touchdown, he is going to have to keep on going and is going to have to go far enough. A lot of people go, but I have seen people come up short, not go far enough to get the touchdown. A lot of Christians move forward in the Lord, but they do not go far enough. They are not willing to put forth the extra energy and effort it will take to get the reward.

A football player has to decide, "I am going to get that yardage even if I have to run over three people rather than two."

Well, a Christian has to decide, "I am going to get that prize of the Lord even if I have to run over three demons instead of two."

Don't go part way. Go all the way. It takes that sense of trusting God and that reckless abandon in Him that says, "I am going for it whole hog. I am going to get it. I am going to get that touchdown. I am going to do what God has called me to do. I am going to be where He wants me to be, say what He wants me to say."

That is something a lot of preachers never understand. They are not willing to get up in the pulpit and say what needs to be said. They are not willing to pay the price. There are certain ballplayers over the years that I have really admired. A fellow by the name of Jim Taylor used to play for the Green Bay Packers. I used to love to watch him play. There would be at least three guys on every play who would try to tackle that dude, but he would just keep on going.

A lot of times I think of that type of thing in spiritual warfare. You have to have the tenacity of a bulldog. You have to duck your head and keep on going. Even when it does not look right, when it seems as if you are not going to get anywhere, you have to just keep on going. Don't go part way, go far enough. Do it one step at a time. You do not have to make a touchdown every time, but you do need to make some first downs.

A lot of you think, "Just because I didn't make a touchdown this time, I didn't win." Well, bless God, make a few first downs! Keep stacking up those first downs, and eventually you are going to make the touchdown. Some of you get discouraged and disappointed, "I didn't make it the first time." So what? Make the first down and go on.

When I used to play football, one of the things we used to do in practice when we got physically tired was to play "brother-in-law." That means, one of us would say to the other, "I'll hit you real easy if you'll hit me real easy." We would just go through the motions in other words. We were not really going to work at the game. When it came time to block, we would just kind of lean into the other one. We were not willing at that time to pay the price.

The coach wanted to cure us, so he caught me and another fellow "brother-in-lawing" one day and made us take off our helmets and kiss one another. Yuch! Man, that was tough! I mean, it was a bad scene anyway you looked at it! We knew that it would take going at the game in a rough way to develop and mature, and yet we didn't do it. Therefore, we placed ourselves in a position to lose simply because we did not do what we knew to do.

The Bible says, **Therefore to him that knoweth to do good, and doeth it not, to him it is sin** (James 4:17). If Christians ever understand that God wants to bless them, that it is His desire, then they will do what is necessary to keep going long enough to get in position to receive those blessings and rewards.

I began to want all of the benefits of playing football, so I began to really try, and I attained some level of success and thoroughly enjoyed it.

Get Free

The next thing I noticed watching the Super Bowl was that when the tight end went out to receive that pass, he had to get free.

I have seen people so bound up in the affairs of life, so bottled up in things rather than being where they ought to be, that they could not get in position to receive from God. I have seen people get tied up with their jobs and never come to church. I have seen people bound up with habits to the point that their faith was blocked to receive from God. I have seen people so hung up on smoking, for example, that it brought such condemnation to them they felt they could not receive the Holy Spirit.

When a football player goes out to receive that pass, he has to shake everything off and get out there in the open. He has to get free.

You ask, "How do I get free?"

Just like the tight end, you have to fight to get free. You have to fight the faith fight — "by faith I'm free of that; by faith I will do this" — and so forth. If you let your past keep you bound up so that you cannot move forward, you will never get in a position to receive. If you think, "Well, I have always been this way; I guess I always will," you will never change.

If the Son therefore shall make you free, ye shall be free indeed (John 8:36). Allow the Spirit of God to set you free so that you can move on out and get into a position to receive the blessings that God wants you to have, the ultimate of what He would have you do.

You have to get free, free of all the binding forces that come against you. Habits, the past, fears, doubts: shake them all off and get free of them.

Get Into Position

Then, another thing I noticed was that when the tight end got free of entanglements, he got into position to receive. Think about Moses for a minute. Think about him from a natural standpoint.

Moses had certain rights and privileges because he was the adopted son of Pharaoh. He was in position for certain rewards, certain benefits, certain blessings in life. No doubt, he was God's man of the hour, the deliverer, a type and shadow of the Christ Who was to come. Physically he was to lead the Israelites out of bondage just as Jesus leads all who will follow Him out of bondage.

But Moses moved too quickly. He got off to the side and out of position. The minute he got out of position and killed an Egyptian in order to try and bring to pass what God had said, it cost him — and the people he was to lead — forty years. He had to spend forty years on the sidelines. That is a pretty good-sized penalty!

Even though he was penalized, he was still on the team and still God's key player. After the forty years of maturing and developing, God moved him back onto the field. Moses came face to face with the Coach in the burning bush.

Some young Christians get to thinking they can go out and set the world on fire immediately. And, like my grandfather used to say, "A little wild fire is better than no fire at all." I mean, it is awful hard to burn an old, wet blanket. I would rather have people in the church who need to be tamed down and put on the bench for a while than people who are just sitting there, wondering where to go or what to do.

Let the Spirit of God set a fire inside you, then look for that position and start moving toward it. Do whatever it takes to get into a position to receive from God.

So what is the right position? Well, when that ballplayer got free of the rest of the players and got into position to receive that pass, *he turned to face the ball.* He caught some over his shoulder, he caught a few looking back, but he did the best when he faced the quarterback. He was then in a position to solidly receive.

Look at the Play Face to Face

Most people are trying to receive looking back over their shoulders, on the run, rather than in a face-to-face experience with God. You will find that you can hang on to the things of God so much better when you turn face to face and look at Him and say, "I want it." Then you can hold your arms out in the open and receive what He wants to give you.

One of the best ways to get into position is to come face to face with Jesus. That experience has a way of dispelling the powers of darkness and putting you into a position to receive like you never have been in before. I can see all through the Word of God where different people paid the price to get into position. Most people get themselves into the wrong position.

You can walk out there in the street, into the middle of traffic, and get yourself in a position to get killed. Spiritually speaking, a lot of Christians have gotten themselves into some stupid positions, and the devil has taken advantage of it to literally kill them or to kill their Christian growth or testimony. They have not known how to believe God to get themselves out of that position. When you see you are out of position, you need to turn around.

An old-time Pentecostal preacher put it this way: "One thing about it, you have to get under the spout where the glory comes out." Buckets of blessings are pouring out of Heaven, but you have to get under the bucket to receive any of them. Right? It is not just a matter of whether God is pouring out blessings, but it is a matter of whether you are in a position to receive them.

The Spirit of God is being poured out in this land today in a tremendous way, yet there are churches that are dead and dry and do not know what is happening. Why? They are not in a position to receive from God.

Going to a university or a Bible school can put you into a position to receive — if that is where God wants you. But then you have to do the other things — mature, develop, do what has to be done to win the prize. It is not enough just to get on the team. Your whole attitude is what tells the tale about whether you make it or not. I have seen a lot of people who did real well in the Lord's work who did not go to a place of formal training!

We need to turn face to face if we are going to receive from God in great confidence and fullness and then hang on to what we have received.

Find Your Own Position

The last thing involved in this "Super Bowl message" is finding your own position. Find out where God wants *you*. Preachers or other leaders of the Church cannot dictate to you and try to tell you where your place is — only God can do that. We can tell you to search for it and tell you the steps to go through while you are searching. We can tell you to be determined, to be diligent, but only you and the Lord know your place.

The reason many of you receive blessings is because you made quality decisions to find that place and put yourselves in it, no matter what it took. When you are at the right place at the right time, right things happen. If you think God is not working on some kind of schedule and program, you had better think again! He has an ultimate goal to finish the game, but He wants each one of His people in position. We are team members, and God wants each of us positioned right. I am glad that I have found my place. I am glad that you can find your place.

Many of us are in the Body, but we need to grow into the positions where God wants us. The growing process is a natural, normal thing, if you just let God do it. The Apostle Paul did that. He started out as a teacher. Later, he referred to himself as a prophet and still later as an apostle. He grew and changed positions in the Body.

I began in a helps ministry, then I was a teacher, then a pastor. I have changed positions, but in each position I was placed to receive God's blessings because, at that time, I was where He wanted me.

So you have to get on the team, then you have to go and work. You have to accomplish the goal. It takes discipline, it takes skill and it takes development. For the higher blessings, the higher gifts, it takes all these things.

You have much reward just by being in the family, or on the team, of God. It is your rightful inheritance. But if you want the satisfaction of the higher rewards, the crown of the winner, you have to work for it.

You say, "You mean that we are supposed to work, to earn something from God?" Yes, I certainly do, and no, your work will not get you into Heaven. It might get someone else in, however. The grace of God is what will get me, and you, into Heaven. But my working, being diligent, being faithful, developing skills, getting in the action, going far enough to win, getting free of entanglements could determine whether somebody else makes it or not. My being in a position to give them the good news could mean the difference between someone receiving Jesus as Lord or going to hell.

You see, winning the game is not dependent on one person or two persons. It is dependent on everyone in the Body being willing and obedient to do their part, to move forth and say, "Yes, Lord, you asked me to do that, and I am willing and obedient to do it." It depends on people not saying, "Well, someone else can do that job better than I can."

You do not need to talk yourself out of the plan of God. You need to be in a position to receive. Receive today!

Key 4
Manage the Whole You

Key 4
Manage the Whole You

And the very God of peace sanctify you wholly; and I pray God your whole spirit and soul and body be preserved blameless unto the coming of our Lord Jesus Christ.

1 Thessalonians 5:23

The three main keys to power that I have given you so far are vision, communication and positioning. The fourth key is simple. It is called self-management.

In 1 Thessalonians 5:23, Paul talks about the self as having three parts — spirit, soul and body. As a matter of fact, he prays that the church be sanctified wholly and preserved until Christ returns. The word, *wholly*, speaks of fullness and completeness.[1] In other words, you cannot just emphasize the body and expect to be whole and complete. No! You must feed and nurture the *whole* man in order to rise to the full potential God created you to fulfill.

Some people may wonder why they are not spiritually strong. Maybe it is because they feed their body three hot meals a day and their spirit only one cold snack a week. We must put something into our spirit before we can expect anything to come out. If we are not putting anything in, no matter how smart we think we are, nothing is going to come out. There have been a lot of people on a spiritual fast and, as a result, are getting no where. To get where we need to be and to do what God wants us to do, we must learn to manage ourselves *wholly* — spirit, soul and body.

---

[1]*Webster's*, s.v. "wholly."

Managing Your Spirit

Since God works from the inside out, He starts with your spirit man. When you stop and think about managing the inward man, you find out that it is a lot like managing the outward man. To have a healthy outward man or body, there are three fundamental things involved: good food, exercise and rest. To have a healthy inward man or spirit, the same three fundamentals are involved: good food, exercise and rest.

Feed Your Spirit

The Word of God is good food for your spirit man, and the *good* food of the Word is what you need. You could take the Word and just eat what you enjoyed. You could make it by on a junk food diet. But to be healthy, you have to eat the right foods. You have to eat a balanced diet. So the way you manage your spirit is by feeding on the *good* Word of God. That is why you get books and tapes. That is why you go to church. That is why you forsake not the assembling of yourselves together. In other words, it is a part of self-management.

If you don't go to church and you don't stay built up in God's Word, you will lose sight of the image of the vision that God gave to you. It won't be long until you will start blaming God because the vision isn't coming to pass the way He said. But it isn't God's fault! You just didn't manage yourself, and the power was cut down. You have to manage yourself. You have to manage your spirit man and continually feed him.

Exercise Your Spirit

Do you know what happens if all you ever do is eat and never exercise? You will have problems, big problems, with your body. The same thing is true spiritually. There are many people who feed on the Word of God but who never pray in the Holy Ghost. Then they wonder why they are not spiritually strong. We have to exercise our spirit man by praying in the Holy Ghost.

In Jude 20, it says, **But ye, beloved, building up yourselves....** Notice he says, **...building up yourselves on your most holy faith....** He doesn't say building up your faith because that comes from the Word. Instead he says, **building up yourselves on your most holy faith.** By doing what? **...praying in the Holy Ghost.**

You send your kids to school to build mental muscles. You work out with weights to build physical muscles, but you pray in tongues to build spiritual muscles. You don't build physical muscles by lifting a barbell once. No, it requires continuous effort, and it takes a while before you can see the muscle growing. After a few weeks or months, you can begin to see a difference. If you will stay with it, in a year or two, you can actually develop all the muscles you want.

The same is true when you pray in the Spirit. You may pray five minutes and not notice being any stronger. Stay with it. You have just begun. It must become a way of life, not just an experience you are trying for the moment. Before you get out of bed in the morning, you ought to sing and pray in tongues. In fact, it wouldn't hurt if you went to sleep praying in tongues.

What I am saying is that once you receive the infilling in the Holy Spirit then you need to continue in it. You don't pray in tongues once then never pray in tongues again. No, you should be filled with the Spirit daily. This is what the apostles did.

All through the book of Acts, it mentions the apostles being "filled with the Spirit." I am not a Greek scholar, but I have been told by those who are that the tense of this verb, "be filled," would be better translated by the phrase, "continually being filled."[2]

---

[2]Jack W. Hayford, ed., *Spirit-Filled Life Bible* (Nashville, Tennessee: Thomas Nelson Publishers, 1991), p. 1794.

The first evidence of being filled with the Spirit is your faith, and the first outward evidence is speaking in tongues. This is the same evidence that occurred at the initial outpouring of the Holy Spirit on the Day of Pentecost. Being filled with the Spirit and then never speaking in tongues after the initial evidence is like taking a drink and then thinking you never need water again. Just because you had one drink does not mean you will never need water again. It is not enough to take one drink of the Holy Spirit. You have to keep on drinking.

It is a daily process to satisfy the thirst of your spirit and to sustain your spirit so you can grow. But as you do, the power you need to fulfill the vision God has given you will increase, and you will be able to see it through.

My wife, Pat, and I have been married over thirty-five years, and one of the reasons our marriage survived in the early years was that we would take one another in our arms and pray in tongues together. Through this, God built a bond and a dynamic love between us.

When the storms of life came, when my stupidity and ignorance as a young man tried to overtake me, I had learned to give place to the Holy Spirit, and He was able to see me through hard times and stupid mistakes. The first seven years were like hell on earth, and I created most of them through immaturity and stupidity. But the Spirit of God kept working with me and worked all these things out in my life.

So I know by personal experience that the Holy Spirit can change your life, turn it around and resolve the problems. The key is to remain continually filled with the Spirit. If you will stay continually filled with His Spirit, then you will be able to reach down inside your own spirit and draw from His power as you need it.

Rest Your Spirit

Rest is another essential part of spiritual health. You need to rest so that you don't wear yourself out and become run down. You may be thinking about the bills that are due or the deadlines at work that need to be met, and you may be asking yourself, "How do you rest when all of this is going on?" You rest by faith and cast all your care upon Him. (1 Pet. 5:7.)

"Well, how do you do that?" It is easy. You start by praying in the Holy Ghost. "What happens when you pray in the Holy Ghost?" You become more God-conscious than you are problem-conscious. When you lose sight of your problems, you are more conscious of God and are more likely to become aware of the solution because He is the One with the solutions, not the problems! When you have given your problem to Him and you know that He has the solution, it is easy to rest. Do you see that?

Isaiah 28:12 talks about God speaking to His people with stammering lips and another tongue saying, This is the rest that will cause the weary to rest. This is the refreshing. Why? Because when you are praying in tongues, the Holy Ghost is the One Who is praying through you. Because He is a part of the Godhead, He knows all things and is able to pray for things that you don't even know about. But you can be sure that He will always pray in line with the will of God. So when He finishes praying through you, you will know that you will have prayed the perfect prayer and covered all the bases.

If you don't feel a peace in your heart when you finish praying then you need to continue praying until you have a peace. When you pray until you have peace, then you can know that you know whatever you were praying about is settled. When you have a peace in your heart, then you can rest in your faith knowing that the rest is up to Him.

Managing Your Soul

When you speak in tongues, your spirit gets built up, but your mind doesn't get a thing out of it. For your mind to be built up spiritually and be renewed, you need the interpretation of what has been said in tongues. So when you pray in tongues, you need to ask for the interpretation as well.

Renew Your Mind by Interpreting Your Tongues

How do you interpret your tongues? The way to begin operating in the interpretation of tongues is to pray or sing in tongues until you have a sense of satisfaction in the spirit, then stop and begin listening for words in English. Then begin to pray or sing out loud with the "understanding" as Paul said in 1 Corinthians 14:15. The most important thing is to start speaking out those words. Even if it doesn't sound right in the beginning, keep on going. The more you do it the more sure you will become. Your mind will be refreshed because it will know what the Spirit is saying.

Oral Roberts built a multi-million dollar university that is blessing thousands upon thousands of lives today because he understood this principle. Everything about Oral Roberts University — its design, the buildings, the principles by which it operates, the people who are there and their job responsibilities — came to Brother Roberts through his speaking in tongues and then interpreting in English what the Holy Spirit was saying.

His Holy Spirit is the same as yours, and you can do the same if you are in the process of being constantly filled. You can pray out the answers for your business, your marriage difficulties, your problems with your children or any other problems. By praying and interpreting your tongues, you can get directions from headquarters that are not just mental and half-heard but that are clear and straightforward.

There are times when I get so busy running all the things I am involved in that it seems I can't stand any more details. So I just turn around, walk out of the office and go home. I walk through the house singing in tongues, singing the interpretation and praising God. I get myself built up again and am ready to go.

I couldn't face the problems I have to face without this. You don't deal with hundreds of churches, a publishing company, Bible schools and thousands of ministers without facing some problems. There has to be somewhere to go for answers, somewhere to go for comfort and some way to get the mind of God on how to solve problems and how to do some things.

If you will enter into that other dimension where you can pray things out, you won't have to wander around questioning everybody else asking, "Is this God's will for me?" You will know what God's will is because you will know His voice and will be able to make the decision to follow it.

God wants you to know that you know that you know what His will is. He is not a hit-or-miss, could-be, might-be, maybe-so, hope-so God. He is an absolute God. He is known as "the Great I Am." He doesn't offer us uncertainties. He offers us surety, absoluteness, guarantees. When you start seeing Him in that light, you will be more sure of yourself because you are sure of His voice. Other people may think it is cockiness, but really it is confidence in Someone greater than yourself.

Renew Your Mind by Meditating on His Word

Another way to renew your mind is to feed on God's Word. The Word of God is God's will. When you feed on His Word, His will becomes your will, and that is how you develop will power. One way to feed on God's Word is by meditating on it. I have had people say to me, "I don't know how to meditate." Yes, you do. You know how to worry, don't you? Then you know how to meditate because worry is just negative meditation. When you meditate on something, you think about it over and over and over again. When you meditate on God's Word, you think about it over and over and over again.

There are a number of different ways that people use to meditate on the Word. I like to meditate by reading the verse aloud. Usually I will take one word at a time and emphasize it when I read the verse. I will think on that one word for a while and mull it over in my mind then read the verse again and emphasize the next word.

Take for example Philippians 4:19. Have you ever confessed that verse? I have done overtime confessing that verse, but it seemed like it didn't get inside my spirit until I started meditating on it. Then it started becoming real to me and began to change my life.

Notice that Paul begins Philippians 4:19 saying, **But my God....** *My* God is personal. He is not my granddaddy's, not my daddy's, not my uncle's, not my brother's, not my sister's, not my mother's, but He is *my* God. It gets personal, doesn't it?

As I thought about it over and over, it began to sink in. **But my *God*....** Well, whose God? *El Shaddai*, the many Breasted One, the One Who has a full supply, the One Who never runs out, the One Who owns the silver, the gold and the cattle on a thousand hills, the One to Whom the fullness thereof belongs.

My God *shall*.... Not hope so, maybe so, might be or could be. No, He shall! *Shall* is a certain assertion. There is no question that it will happen.

My God shall *supply*.... And does He have a supply! I mean everything belongs to Him. He is not lacking. He is not without. Bless God, **my God shall supply *all*,** not a little bit, not half. No, **my God shall supply all *your* need.** Glory to God, this verse is talking about your need. It is talking about my need!

My God shall supply all your *need.* And do I have need. I have need like you have never seen need. Are you following what I am saying here?

As I began to pound that verse into my spirit, as I began to think about it and do it, it began to come alive to me. Now what was I doing? I was renewing my mind. I was managing my soul. I was making my mind line up with the revelation as it flowed out of my spirit so that my mind would become effective and would work *with* my spirit rather than against it.

Too many times we walk around looking for somebody to agree with us for money, for healing or for a particular problem to be solved. If we would just get our mind and our spirit in agreement, we would find all the help we needed. I am not against getting somebody to agree with you, don't misunderstand me, but it would help for you to get in agreement with yourself.

Meditation, like the interpretation of tongues, helps you to get your mind renewed so it is in line with your spirit and can help to bring to pass God's will in your life. Renewing your mind is a process and doesn't happen overnight. Sometimes, in the process, your emotions will give you problems because they are so accustomed to lining up with the unrenewed mind which goes by what it sees rather than the spirit which operates in faith. The mind, will and emotions are all a part of your soul, and you are the one who is responsible for seeing that they stay submitted to the Spirit of God.

Deal With Your Emotions

Through the years, I have found that praying or singing in the Holy Ghost has helped me to deal more effectively with my emotions. Paul, in his letter to the Ephesian church, exhorts them to speak to themselves in psalms and hymns and spiritual songs and to sing and make a melody in their heart to the Lord. (Eph. 5:19.)

Exhorting or speaking to yourself is a Biblical pattern. David did it. The Bible says he encouraged himself in the Lord. (1 Sam. 30:6.) If you don't encourage yourself, many times there is no one else around to do it. If you don't encourage yourself in the Lord, He is not going to comfort you. Many of you are not spiritual babies anymore, and He expects you to learn to walk. Begin encouraging yourself in the Lord by reminding yourself what God has to say in His Word about you or your situation.

You may even want to speak to yourself and to God in other tongues. This is a way that you can pour out your heart before Him and really let Him know what is going on inside. Sometimes your mind may not even understand why your emotions are acting the way they are, but God's Spirit, which knows all things, dwells in you and can help you to communicate to Him what is going on. When you are hurt, when somebody has said something nasty or hurtful, those are the times to pray in tongues.

You will find that as you speak to yourself in other tongues you may even begin to sing spiritual songs. Since God is the author of the spiritual song, He gives you the words and the tune as you go along, and it comes out of your heart, your spirit man.

What we sing on the spur of the moment by the Spirit of God is what the Spirit is prompting us to declare at that instant and will speak to those who hear it. These are songs written not to bless us but to worship and praise *Him*. Sometimes, you may start out by speaking to yourself and sing yourself right into victory, singing and making melody unto the Lord.

I remember when my Daddy died. Naturally sorrow came. It wasn't just that I was thinking of losing my Daddy for my sake, but it was the fact that my mother was going to be affected. My children and grandchildren were going to be affected. So the sorrow I had was a godly sorrow. But, I knew if I wasn't careful that my sorrow would turn into grief. And grief started to try and come, and the only way that I could overcome it was to begin to sing a spiritual song.

So, at first, I began to sing in the Spirit. After a while, my mind quieted down, and I began to hear words in English and started singing the interpretation. When the Holy Ghost in your spirit starts to quicken you with the words of the Spirit of God to your spirit then your emotions start to feel the affect of it, and He begins to quicken your mortal body. So by the time I walked out of the room, I was actually dancing and shouting.

I had experienced that day the real heartbeat of God because He is looking for worshipers who will worship Him with their whole heart. John 4:23 says,

> **But the hour cometh, and now is, when the true worshippers shall worship the Father in spirit and in truth: for the Father seeketh such to worship him.**

The hour has come, and now is, when He is looking for those who will worship Him. If He can find somebody who will worship Him, that person will come to a place of freedom, victory, liberty and joy because worship will bring him into the presence of the Lord, and in the presence of the Lord, there is the fullness of joy. When you get full of the joy of God, then you have the strength to do whatever He wants you to do.

Really, until you learn how to worship, you are not even capable of doing a work for the Lord. Without worship, you are limited because, somewhere along the way, fear will overtake you. You will not be able to do what God wants you to do because you have not entered into His presence and received the strength or direction you need.

The Holy Spirit is here to make us worshipers, but we have to avail ourselves to His help. It is up to us to allow

Him to fill us every day. We are the ones who need to keep on speaking in other tongues. We are the ones who need to stir up the gifts, and He is the One Who will keep us full. You can tell something is full when it runs over. You can tell somebody is full when tongues just come bubbling out of their mouth.

When you understand this Biblical pattern for victory, you can sing and shout every day of your life. You can stay in a place of victory rather than sinking into despair. There is no reason for you to have "blue Mondays." There is no reason to ever be despondent or down. There is no reason to feel defeated because you have the Holy Ghost living inside of you, and He will help you out.

Managing Your Body

So you must manage your spirit, your soul and your body. If you manage your body, you are going to have a powerful business, but if you don't manage your body, eventually you won't even be able to do business. Are you following me?

For years, I pushed forward in spiritual things and managed my mind, but for a long time, I wouldn't manage my body and, as a result, started to have physical battles. They weren't major battles between life and death, but I knew that somewhere down the road, if I didn't hurry up and manage my own body, I wasn't going to be what God wanted me to be and would end up getting slowed down.

The body is important. There is no doubt about it. But there are a lot of people in this society and in this hour who have become excessive. They have gotten so caught up in their body that they have almost begun to worship their body. There are more diets out there than you can shake a stick at. There is more exercise equipment being sold now than ever before. People are buying lifetime memberships to fitness centers so they can work out. I mean, they are conscious of their body and what they are doing with their body. They are conscious of what they are putting in their mouth and what they are eating.

There was a time in my life that I ate just whatever I could get my hands on. I wasn't conscious of what I was eating. Like one fellow said, I was on a see-food diet! I would see food and eat it. I would stay right there, you know, until it was finished.

At one point though, I even tried to lose weight, but I could not get a vision for it. I worked on it, but I didn't get in bondage over it like some did who concluded that you couldn't do anything for God because you were a certain height or a certain weight. You don't need that kind of bondage. What you need to be is who and what God wants you to be. In other words, you need to be in the fashion and form that He is dealing with you about. You need to be what He has planted in your spirit regardless of what others may say.

The last few times I turned on the television at home there was a certain channel that dealt just with the physical. They either had an exercise program going or a skin care program that told ladies more about putting on make-up. Personally I am not against ladies wearing make-up. Some of them need it! I once heard a fellow put it this way, "If an old barn needs paint, you would paint it, wouldn't you? Well, you ought to at least do that for your wife."

In other words, there is nothing wrong with wearing a little bit of makeup, and I am not going to put down ladies who do, but what I am against is majoring on minors and minoring on majors. Whether you wear make up or don't wear make up isn't a major issue, but what you put on the inside is. The Bible says very clearly not to spend *all* of your time on the outward adorning of the body, but to adorn yourself with a meek and quiet spirit in the hidden man of your heart. (1 Pet. 3:3,4.)

Don't worship your body. Worship God and present your body a living sacrifice, holy and acceptable unto God. This is your reasonable service. (Rom. 12:1.) God wants you to get your body under control, but He doesn't want your body to control you.

The Result of Self-Management

Once you can manage yourself, you are more able to manage the world around you. Why? Because as you are faithful to manage what He has given you, He will give you more. You are just like your Father. He manages His world, and you manage the world He has given you. (Gen.1:26-28.)

I know in my life there came a time when God began to entrust me with other young men to train. In the process, I learned to accept them where they were at and realized that if I gave them the Word of God, they would change and grow into what they needed to become. Because I accepted them where they were at, I was able to empower them. That is what a leader does. He empowers people. He motivates and inspires people to grow and learn through their efforts so they can translate their vision into reality. Your vision then becomes the vehicle for their personal growth. As time went on, He gave me more to manage, and what I started with has grown and multiplied. Why? Because I was faithful to manage what God had blessed me with in the beginning.

For me, the vision that God gave me has become the vehicle that has allowed Fred Price, Charles Capps and many others to publish their books. It has allowed their vision to grow and to become a reality. They had the truth down inside of them, but the vision I had was to get that truth out to the people, and God has used Harrison House as that vehicle. In other words, my vision was a vehicle to carry their vision. I hope you are carrying something worthwhile of someone else.

I had a vision and a desire for a family, a good family. I had a vision for a marriage, a good marriage. Now, you see, that marriage has become the vehicle that has provided me the children and the family that I had desired.

God wants to put together vehicles for our life to carry us into all the areas that He wants us to be in, to do all the things He wants us to do. Don't see yourself coming up short. He has no plans for failure. Manage yourself wholly — spirit, soul and body. Follow *His* pattern, and your life will be a powerful life.

Conclusion
Fulfill the Vision

Conclusion

Fulfill the Vision

There are four keys to power. They are vision, communication, position and self-management. As you begin to use these keys, you will be able to unlock from within you His power and to do all He has called you to do.

Some of you are already using these keys and are well on your way to fulfilling His plan for your life while others of you have found yourself saying, "Lord, will I ever be in the place You want me to be? Will I ever accomplish what You want me to do?" If you find yourself asking questions like these, then the following word I received through tongues and interpretation will speak to you:

Many have been confused, and some have thought, "I have been misused." But it was misunderstanding that was in the mind because you didn't realize that you were born of another kind. You did not realize and know the Spirit of God had made a rich and powerful deposit in you, so you failed to communicate it so it would come on through and become effectual and begin to work the right way. You got confused and doubted and got into dismay, and you said, "Lord, will I ever be in the place You want me to be? Will I ever accomplish what You want me to do?"

And the Spirit of God would say, "It's time for you to correct some things, but My power will come on through. So if you will arise and begin to speak the words that I have given unto your heart and be faithful to that and from that never depart, I shall construct, rearrange and cause everything to become clear and sound and very plain so that it will not be confusing to your heart or to your mind. I will cause you to realize and recognize that I'm working by My Spirit and My plan. It is divine. So it will readjust. It will realign, and it will begin to become powerful and strong and mighty, just for your life.

If you'll just do what I'm telling you, I'll eliminate the confusion, the frustration and the strife. I will correct it and make it right and cause you to be onward on your goal. So realize that now is the time to come back to that place to where you can say, "I know that I know." Then there will be peace and rest and joy forevermore. Then I will open up to you that door so I can bring you to where you are in My full employ.

So hearken to My voice and hear what I would say to you in this hour because I intend to show Myself strong and demonstrate My glory and My power.

I believe in the days to come God is wanting there to be the springing up of *His* power and *His* glory and that He is going to send a strong wave of His Spirit to bring it forth. The question you have to ask yourself is, "Do I want to be a part of it? Do I want to participate?"

Personally I want to be a part of it and to participate in it. I want to see God sweep through this whole nation in a way that we have never seen before. But it is going to take some people who are committed to having a powerful life, a powerful marriage and a powerful ministry.

I don't mind telling you that I intend to live a powerful life. When I leave this world, the world is going to know that I was here because I am going to leave an impact on this world. Somebody may say, "That's ego." No, that is determination. I am not living my life based on ego. I am living my life based on the will of God. He has told me to go into all the world and preach the Gospel to every creature, and that is what I will do.

Some years back, I set up a publishing company. Day by day we have been faithful to the vision God has given me. Now almost twenty years later approximately fifty million books have passed through just this one publishing company. Whether you know it or not, that is powerful, and lives are being affected. Give me another ten years, and I will affect more people than you ever dreamed of.

Some people may have said that it couldn't be done. But it is too late. It is already done. Don't tell me not to seek after power because I intend to use every ounce of it for the glory of God. Don't tell me you can't do what God has called you to do. He has given you the keys to all the power you need. If you use those keys, your life will change along with many others.

Don't draw back from His power because when you are powerful, the church will be powerful. When the church is powerful, it can affect a whole city. When the whole city is powerful, then the whole county can be powerful. When the whole county is powerful, then the whole state can be powerful. When the whole state is powerful, then the whole nation can be powerful. When the whole nation is powerful, then the whole world will be affected. But it all begins with the power of God within you and within me.

Revival is already here, but we are yet to see the fullness of it, the springing up in the power of it. That, of course, will take an individual decision on your part and a corporate decision on our part. But only *you* can decide to live your life with or without the power of God.

It is my hope that you will decide to live your life with the power of God, to follow the vision He has placed in your heart, communicate it to others so it can become effectual, get into the right position so you can receive His blessings and learn to manage yourself so the vision can be maintained. Unlock the dynamic power of God within you today by putting into practice in your life the four keys to power.

Buddy Harrison is a man walking after love with an apostolic vision for what God is doing today. He moves in the gifts of the Spirit with sensitivity and understanding. He is Founder and President of Faith Christian Fellowship International Church, Inc. and Harrison House, Inc. in Tulsa, Oklahoma. He has authored several books.

As a small boy, Buddy was healed of paralyzing polio. More than 25 years ago he answered the call of God on his life. He is gifted vocally and began his ministry in music and the office of helps. He became Office Manager for Kenneth E. Hagin Ministries and for several years pioneered many areas as Administrator/Office Manager.

In November, 1977, the Lord instructed Buddy to start a family church, a Bible teaching center and a world outreach in Tulsa, Oklahoma. He has obeyed the Spirit of God whatever the cost. Through his obedience, Faith Christian Fellowship was born with 165 people in January, 1978. Now there are more than 373 FCF churches worldwide.

Buddy and his wife, Pat, are known around the world for their anointed teachings from the Word of God, and for their ability to communicate principles from the Word with a New Testament love. Buddy attributes any success he has to obeying the Spirit of God and living the Word.

While in Israel, the Lord spoke to him to serve as pastor to pastors and ministers. His goal is to aid ministers in the spiritual and in the natural. Ministers around the world have received blessings through Buddy's apostolic ministry since he obeyed the vision given in Israel. Under his direction, FCF has grown to become a lighthouse for other Word and Faith churches. Today over 1,250 ministers are affiliated/associated or licensed/ordained through FCF.

For a list of cassette tapes
by Buddy Harrison
or for other information,
write:

Buddy Harrison
P. O. Box 25443
Tulsa, OK 74153

*Please include your prayer requests and comments
when you write.*

Other Books by Buddy Harrison

How To Raise Your Kids in Troubled Times

Petitioning for the Impossible
The Prayer of Supplication

Understanding Authority for Effective Leadership

Getting in Position to Receive

Maintaining a Spirit-Filled Life

Just Do It

Count It All Joy
Eight Keys to Victory in
Times of Temptations, Test, and Trials
Coauthored by Van Gale

The Force of Mercy
The Gift Before and Beyond Faith
Coauthored by Michael Landsman

Available from your local bookstore
or from:

HARRISON HOUSE
P. O. Box 35035
Tulsa, OK 74153

The Harrison House Vision

Proclaiming the truth and the power
Of the Gospel of Jesus Christ
With excellence;

Challenging Christians to
Live victoriously,
Grow spiritually,
Know God intimately.